in
the
news™

HUMAN TRAFFICKING

Joyce Hart

ROSEN PUBLISHING®

New York

Dedicated to all silent victims

Published in 2009 by The Rosen Publishing Group, Inc.
29 East 21st Street, New York, NY 10010

Library of Congress Cataloging-in-Publication Data

Hart, Joyce, 1954–
Human trafficking / Joyce Hart.—1st ed.
    p. cm.—(In the news)
Includes bibliographical references and index.
ISBN-13: 978-1-4358-5038-5 (library binding)
ISBN-13: 978-1-4358-5366-9 (pbk)
ISBN-13: 978-1-4358-5372-0 (6 pack)
1. Human trafficking. 2. Human trafficking—Prevention. I. Title.
HQ281.H38 2008
364.15—dc22

                                                                2008014946

Manufactured in Malaysia

On the cover: Clockwise from top left: Child soldiers in Sierra Leone are released to United Nations officials; children protest against child labor and human trafficking in New Delhi, India; boys as young as five years old are forced to weave rugs in an illegal factory in Attock, Pakistan.

contents

What Is Human Trafficking? 1

What do you think when you hear the word "slavery"? Do you imagine scenes of people stolen from Africa and then being forced to work in cotton fields in the United States? Do you also believe that slavery ended more than a hundred years ago? Well, think again. Slavery is happening right now. It is taking place in almost every country of the world. In fact, there is a good chance that modern-day slaves live not too far from where you live. According to a 2008 report from the U.S. State Department, human trafficking is one of the greatest human rights challenges of this century, both here and abroad.

Definition of Human Trafficking

"Human trafficking" is the term that is used today for modern-day slavery. Like African slaves in past centuries, many people from around the world are being held captive and are forced to work. Some people are physically

Even after the Civil War, many African Americans continued to work under slave conditions.

beaten to make them work. A few others are sold into slavery. Some are kidnapped. But most people are tricked into becoming slaves. They are given false promises of money, new jobs, educations, and better lives. Then the promises are broken. The victims of human trafficking are trapped. Some are even locked behind doors and chained up. Others are told they must continue to work because they owe money to their captors. Or, in some cases, the victims are too young to understand how to free themselves or that they have any right to be free.

Types of Human Trafficking

Victims of human trafficking are forced to labor in various fields. Some are made to act as servants in private homes. Others work in restaurants, doing all the cleanup jobs. People might be forced to work in factories, making things like clothing or rugs. Slave labor can also be found on farms, where people are forced to plant or harvest crops. Women and young girls are often forced to be prostitutes. Some victims are forced to become soldiers and wage war. Young boys, in particular, are trained to handle guns and are then forced to kill those they are told are the enemy. There are many different forms of human trafficking.

Bonded Labor

In bonded labor, a victim borrows money from someone. This victim does not know that the person he has borrowed money from is dishonest. The deal that this victim thinks he is agreeing to is that he can borrow money and then work until the debt is paid off. Although this person works hard for long periods of time, and he pays money to his boss, he is told that he still owes more money. No matter how long this victim works, he is never able to repay the money. The person who lent him the money keeps telling him that he needs to pay more. Because he still owes money, he is forced to work more and to work harder.

Human traffickers use bonded labor to trick their victims. Their victims believe that one day they will be free. They think that if they work hard enough, they will be able to pay back their debt. Some of these people might not have any formal education. They might not know how to do math. They are forced to believe that they still owe money, even when they have really paid off their debt long ago. This form of bonded labor used to occur all over the world. Today, bonded labor is against the law in the United States, but there are some countries that still allow it, such as Nepal, India, and Pakistan.

Involuntary Servitude

Involuntary servitude means that people are forced to work against their will. In this situation, victims work for another person because they are afraid to escape. They believe if they do not do the work, they will be hurt either physically or emotionally. Some human traffickers threaten to beat their victims.

Many cases of involuntary servitude occur when victims are promised a better life in another country. Victims of involuntary servitude are often living in poverty in their home country. They might have no job and little food. They come to a new country illegally

(without the country's permission). The human traffickers sneak them into the new country. Once victims are in the new country, they are forced to do whatever the traffickers tell them to do. This is a particularly prevalent activity among illegal Mexican and other Central and South American immigrants to the United States.

Usually the jobs victims are given are very hard ones. The jobs might even be dangerous. If the victims refuse to do what the traffickers tell them to do, the traffickers threaten to send the victims back to their country.

In some cases, a victim might have agreed to come with the trafficker because her family was starving. She might have believed that if she made a lot of money, she could send it home to her parents. If she is sent back to her country, her family will starve. So, this person continues to work for the human traffickers no matter how difficult the work is because she wants to save her family.

Domestic Servitude

Domestic servants work in people's houses as maids and nannies. They clean the house, take care of young children, and cook the meals for rich people. Most often, domestic servants also live in the houses where they work. Chances are that the victims have been told that if

In Haiti, Tablita, a fourteen-year-old girl, works as a maid but receives no pay.

they work hard, they will earn a lot of money. Or they might be told that they will be allowed to go to school.

Human traffickers often offer women and children these types of jobs. The traffickers know that working in other people's homes is one way to keep the victims hidden. Many times, victims working as domestic servants are not allowed to leave the house. The people they are working for are afraid they might run away. But even when they are allowed out of the house, the victims might speak a different language than the people they meet on the streets. So, they do not know how to tell anyone that they are being abused.

In some very severe cases, domestic servants are locked in their rooms at night. Others are not given enough food to eat. Some are beaten when their employers get angry at them. This often makes them afraid to escape. They might even believe that the beatings they receive are how all servants are dealt with. So, this makes their condition seem normal.

Prostitution

Prostitution is a special category of human trafficking. In this case, the traffickers make money every time their victims, who are mostly women and children, are forced to have sex. Customers "buy" these victims for an hour or so. Sometimes, the victims are made to have sex several times a day. They, too, are often beaten by both their customers and their "employers." Sometimes, they are forced to take drugs to keep them dependent and passive.

Child Labor

Children might be victims of all the different types of human trafficking described above. But because children are so young, defenseless, and generally unaware of their rights, child labor is considered a special cate-gory deserving of special

After being rescued from a brothel in Cambodia, this young girl remains fearful of being recaptured.

protections by legislative bodies and law enforcement agencies worldwide. In some instances, children are taught to kill in order to advance a particular country's war. In other cases, such as in Afghanistan, children work in fields, gathering materials like poppies that will later be made into opium or heroin. Some companies in Africa that produce chocolate are also known to employ large numbers of children. They are made to work long hours in the hot sun. If they receive any money at all, it amounts to not much more than a few pennies. In places like Bangladesh, child labor is often used in factories making things like T-shirts and jeans. Children are also used in the sex trade in places like Bangkok, Thailand.

Many of the children involved in child labor have been kidnapped from their families. Others are orphans who have lost their families to war or to illness.

Human trafficking is particularly damaging to a child. Children are not as well prepared to protect themselves because their experiences are so limited. They have been taught to obey adults, so they will do whatever they are told. Often, these children come from poor families. Chances are they have received no schooling. They do not know how to read. These children may never get the chance to go to school. Even if they escape, their lives will probably not change much. Without an education, they will almost certainly live their lives in poverty.

Where Is Human Trafficking Happening?

Human trafficking occurs in every country of the world. According to the U.S. State Department, human trafficking is the second-largest and the fastest-growing criminal activity in the world. The number of people who are enslaved each year and then transported to another country is estimated to be as high as eight hundred thousand. Of this number, 80 percent of the victims of human trafficking are women and children. Though this number is large, the State Department believes that it is

Sheriff Lee Baca announces a Human Trafficking Awareness Day in Los Angeles, California.

quite possible there could be millions more people who are victims of the modern slave trade.

According to a United Nations report, there could be a total of 12.3 million people trapped in some form of slavery today. Other estimates go as high as 27 million. The reason the numbers vary so much is that it is difficult to uncover all cases of human trafficking, especially when the traffickers and their victims do not cross international borders. If they remain within the borders of their country and are hidden in private houses, public officials may have no knowledge of the victims' situations. In most countries, human trafficking is illegal. Therefore, the traffickers keep their activities as secretive as possible.

So, where exactly is human trafficking happening? It is happening everywhere. Victims of human trafficking are living in countries in Asia, Africa, Europe, North America, and South America. Victims are working in private homes, in factories, and on farms. They are being held captive in big cities and in small towns. In fact, victims of human trafficking are probably being hidden and exploited in your town, maybe even right on your street.

The Causes of Human Trafficking

INGEN:
K (NL)
D (NL)
ERPEN (B)
ESTER (UK)
N (D)

In each country, causes of human trafficking can be different. One country may be suffering the brutalities of a civil war. In such places, young children are often kidnapped and forced to fight. In another country, women might suffer from a lack of civil rights. Young girls might be sold into slavery, often as prostitutes. In yet another country, there might be a great need for cheap labor. In nations like these that need a lot of workers but do not want to pay them a fair wage, children might be forced into labor. Where organized crime (crime mobs, like the Mafia) is very strong, government officials might not be able to stop well-armed and well-funded traffickers from kidnapping people and taking them out of the country.

The most typical causes of human trafficking, however, are poverty, cultural influences, poor education and educational opportunities, corruption and poor law enforcement, lack of awareness, war, high demand for labor, and the huge profits that can be made upon the backs of enslaved and exploited laborers.

Poverty

Poverty causes many people to become victims of human trafficking. Poverty has many different causes. People can become poor because there are no jobs available for them. The lack of jobs might be caused by too many people wanting the same job. Or, maybe there are jobs available, but the person who needs the job does not have the skills and education that the job demands. The reason this person does not have the required education and training might be that there are no schools she can afford to go to or the schools are too far away from her home.

A farming family might suffer from poverty when bad weather destroys the family's crops over several years. The farmer plants his seeds, but the seeds do not grow because of a flood, for instance. Or, maybe there is not enough rain for three years in a row. The farmer then runs out of money and food.

War can also force people out of their homes. This can lead to poverty. The people might have to flee their country in order to stay alive. But when they go to some place that is safe, they may not have any way to earn the money they need to live on. Maybe they do not speak the language of their new country. In addition, because there are so many other people there who have also run away from the war, there are not enough jobs for everyone.

Extreme poverty has forced this family to live right next to train tracks in Jakarta, Indonesia.

Another reason for poverty is based on people overspending the little money they do have. Sometimes, people want to buy things they cannot afford. They might want a television set, for instance. Instead of paying for it with cash, they might use a credit card. They might continue to put more things, like new clothes, DVD players, and jewelry, on their credit cards. Their credit card debt might become so high that they cannot pay their rent or buy food. The family might then become so desperate that they force their children to take jobs arranged by people who deal in human trafficking. They believe they will get out of debt by selling their children. Or, maybe the mother sees no other choice but to sell herself to traffickers.

When people need money, especially for survival, they look for ways to make that money, no matter how desperate. So, when a trafficker comes to their door and promises to give them money, people want to believe the trafficker. The trafficker might make a promise to them. He might say that he will give them money for food if they give him one of their children. Or, he might promise the father a good job if he agrees to go to another country. The trafficker might also tell the mother that he will buy her children new shoes if she works for him in the city.

The problem with all these promises is that human traffickers do not keep them. Or, the traffickers do not explain what kind of job they are really offering. But by the time that the victims discover the traffickers' promises are deceptive, it is too late.

Cultural Influences

Cultural influences are the unwritten rules of a community that affect people's lives. Cultural influences might make people believe they have to dress like everyone around

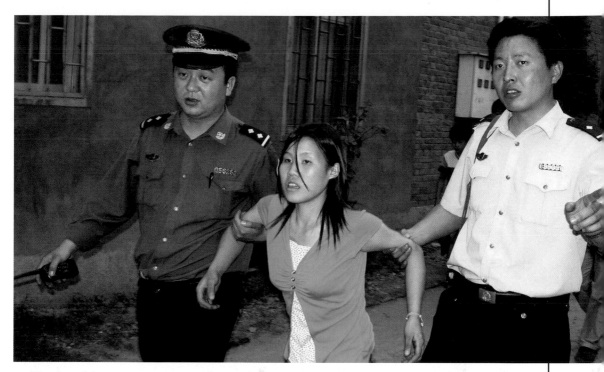

Police in China rescue more than nine thousand kidnapped women and children each year, like this woman who was taken from her home by human traffickers.

them in order to fit in. Cultural influences might also make people believe that one group of people is better than another. These sorts of cultural influences can make some people more susceptible to human trafficking.

In many cultures, men are considered superior to women. Therefore, male children are viewed as more valuable. When a family needs extra money, they might be willing to sell their daughters to human traffickers for a small sum of money. Women born into cultures that make them feel worthless may develop low self-esteem.

Because young girls might not feel good about themselves, they might not complain when people, such as human traffickers, treat them poorly or even beat them. Because of their culture, some women and young girls might even feel like they deserve to be treated this way.

In most cultures, children are taught to obey adults, no matter what. They are trained to do what they are told and not to questions adults' orders. This makes children easy targets for human traffickers. Children, because they are smaller, weaker, and more defenseless than most adults, experience greater fear when someone threatens them. They do not understand that even though they are small, they, too, have rights. But even if children know they have rights, they may not be strong enough to fight for them. This makes children easy prey for people who are dealing in human trafficking. Children are the easiest targets for kidnapping because they are so small, and often they are very trusting of people who are older than they are.

Another way that culture might influence a child is when that culture has a history of child labor practices. Younger members of a family might remember stories that their grandparents and parents have told them about working when they were only five years old. If the grandparents and parents worked when they were children, then the next generations might believe that it is their duty to work also. Even though it is a tradition in a family to put young children to work, this does not mean that it is right. Today, there are many laws against forcing children to work. However, these laws are not always obeyed.

Lack of Education

People who have either limited education or no schooling at all are extremely vulnerable to human trafficking. Education can provide skills that allow a person to work several different kinds of jobs. The more skills a person has, the better chance that person has of finding work. If a person has no education and no special training, his or her chances of finding anything but the lowest-paying jobs are very low. People without training or education will often take any kind of job they can get. This is true even if they have to travel to another country to get the job. Untrained people are usually desperate to find work because jobs that require no training are very hard to find. This means they will be very eager to go along with a person who is dealing in human trafficking. It will be easy to convince this person that a good-paying job is just a few miles away.

Corruption and Weak Enforcement of Laws

Corruption, or dishonesty, among government officials and police of a particular country can make it very easy for human traffickers to conduct their illegal activities. If an official is corrupt, a trafficker can give money to that official and ask the official to keep a secret and not turn the trafficker in. This is known as a bribe. So, even though a country might have rules against human trafficking, the trafficker is not sent to jail. The corrupt official protects the trafficker. The trafficker, even when he is caught abusing his victims, may be allowed to continue his illegal activities as long as he keeps paying the official. Every country is plagued by at least some corruption among those in authority. In some of the worst countries, the police, the judges, and the lawmakers might all be dishonest.

Traffickers can also bribe corrupt immigration officials. When traffickers bring foreigners into a new country, they need special legal documents. The new country they are entering needs to see these documents to approve their admission. Traffickers can pay corrupt immigration officials to make fake ID cards, birth certificates, or passports so the traffickers can bring their victims across the border illegally.

Lack of Awareness

Many people who are victims of human trafficking might have no idea what they are getting into. They might believe everything that human traffickers tell them. They

A corrupt policeman in Nepal forces this man to pay a bribe before he can cross the border.

do not know that these traffickers are lying to them and doing something that is illegal. But even when victims escape and go back to their country and their home, they might be too ashamed to tell anyone in their family or community what has happened to them. Because of this, other people also become victims of human traffickers. If the first victim had talked about what happened to him or her, then other people might question the promises that the traffickers make to them. They might recognize the traffickers for the liars and criminals that they are.

However, it is often the case that the word does not get out. Maybe the victim who escapes is afraid to say anything. Maybe she is afraid that if she talks, the traffickers will kidnap her again or harm her physically. Or, maybe she is scared that the traffickers will hurt her family. Whatever the reason, many people do not talk about their horrible experiences. Because they do not talk about them, other people often do not fully understand the problem of human trafficking or its dangers.

War

War causes a lot of disruption in a country. Parents might be killed, leaving children to take care of themselves without adult help or supervision. In other cases, houses are burned, forcing families to move into refugee camps. These camps are often swarming with traffickers. They know they will find a lot of people there who are in need of help. The traffickers might make promises to rebuild destroyed homes. Or, they might tell people that they will take them to a new country, where they will find peace. Human traffickers can and do promise anything. This does not mean that they will keep those promises once they have captured their newest victims.

In the case of a civil war, when two or more groups from the same country are fighting each other, soldiers often kidnap children and force them to join the fight.

Former child soldiers in Sierra Leone's civil war wait to be turned over to the protection of the United Nations. These children have been forced to kill during civil wars in Africa.

Many of these children are orphans. War to some children might seem like a game, at first. But then they are forced to kill other people. They are also forced to walk for long periods each day. They probably are not fed very much food. They soon discover that war is not a game at all. But if they do not do what their captors tell them to do, they fear that they, too, will be killed.

Civil wars can also cause shortages of food. The lack of food can make people desperate. Starving people are more willing to take any kind of job that someone offers them in order to save their families and fill their empty stomachs.

Demand for Services

A demand for services means that somewhere in the world, someone needs a job to be done. If there is a high demand for services, there will be a high demand for labor. During potato harvest time, for example, there will be a high demand for farmhands. Once the potatoes are fully grown, they must be harvested or they will rot in the ground. Whereas the farmer might have not needed so many workers a few months ago after planting, suddenly that farmer needs a lot of workers and soon.

When there is a demand for services, human traffickers will eagerly fill it with slaves or very low-cost workers. This makes farmers happy, since they don't have to pay high wages but must merely pay the trafficker for his services. In countries that produce a lot of agricultural products, the demand for field workers is great, especially at planting and harvesting times. Fieldwork usually does not pay well. The living conditions are often very poor. Houses that are provided may be falling down. There may not be any heat or water in the houses. Many people might have to sleep in the same room without any beds. But the victims of human trafficking need the money.

And the farmers need the help. So, traffickers supply the workers.

Another example of a demand for low-cost labor occurs in factories. More and more people want to buy clothes that do not cost very much money. In order to keep prices down, owners of some factories need a lot of poorly paid workers. The owners might have prom-ised to ship out thousands of T-shirts to a store in the United States. They must make those shirts as quickly as they can. This causes a demand for services. Human traffickers find new victims and place them in these factories. Under the worst con-ditions in a factory, people are forced to work very long hours each day. They are not paid well and often are not given many breaks in the day.

A young migrant laborer in the Philippines protests new Japanese immigration policies that seek to curb human traf-ficking by cracking down on illegal immigrant laborers.

There is also a growing demand for what is being called sex tourism. Men (and sometimes women) from different parts of the world travel to another country, as if they were on vacation. But what they want to do is have sex with young girls or boys. Human traffickers, knowing that these men will pay a lot of money for prostitutes, entice or kidnap people and force them to go to work for them. This is a particularly notorious practice in parts of Southeast Asia, such as Thailand, but it occurs all over the world.

Huge Profits

There is another major reason for the increasing incidents of human trafficking. It is the money that is made, not by the victims, but by the traffickers. Because human trafficking is an illegal business, there is no sure way to figure out exactly how much money is being made. But people who have been studying this problem do know that the traffickers are making a lot of money. Some studies have estimated that the human trafficking business might be making as much as $9 billion each year.

According to both the U.S. State Department and the United Nations, the business of human trafficking is growing each year. One of the reasons that the business of human trafficking is doing so well is that many countries are not putting human traffickers in jail. Despite the fact that human trafficking is illegal all over the world, victims of human trafficking are too scared to go to court and accuse those who have abused them. Courts cannot put traffickers in jail unless there are witnesses. If no one is willing to point a finger and say that this is the person who abused me, then the courts cannot convict the criminals. So, traffickers are not afraid of being caught. As a result, they keep building their businesses. When other criminally minded people see how much money the traffickers are

Police in Belgium crack down on human traffickers who smuggled more than 12,000 illegal immigrants out of Albania into Britain via trucks in one year.

making, they, too, start their own businesses in turning people into slaves.

The Effects of Human Trafficking

The effects of human trafficking on the individual who has been enslaved can be devastating. First, there is often some form of physical abuse. Victims are often badly beaten so they will do what they are told to do. Sometimes, victims are told that if they do not obey, their families will be hurt or that they will be handed over to immigration authorities. Others may not be physically harmed, but they are abused emotionally. They are made to be afraid of their captors because their captors scare them. They may become fearful of losing their lives. Still other victims are shamed. Their captors tell them that their families will be disgraced once they hear what the victims have done. Victims, even once they are released, may be scarred for life.

There are also other consequences of human trafficking. Many people who have been enslaved are not fed properly. They are not allowed to visit medical professionals. They are also worked so hard that their bodies become weakened. Diseases find easy targets in these victims. The diseases become stronger and begin to spread. The illnesses do not stay confined to only the population of slaves. The diseases can extend to the communities where the slaves live, infecting even larger numbers of people.

The effects of human trafficking also involve those who are making money from dealing in this criminal activity. The traffickers gain power. The more money and power they have, the more people they can enslave. If human trafficking is not stopped, the number of slaves and traffickers will increase every year.

A counselor in the Philippines speaks to a teen who was rescued from a home where she worked as a domestic slave.

Each form of human trafficking presents its own individual problems. Also, the effects of human trafficking on different people can vary. Children, for example, are the most vulnerable part of the population of victims of this illegal activity. The effects of slavery on children can last longer and be more devastating than the effects that adults suffer. There are also different effects on people who are enslaved, depending on what they are forced to do. Women who are forced into the sex trade will suffer physical and emotional effects that are different from men who are forced to work on farms or boys who are made to fight wars.

Physical Effects

There is a wide range of physical effects on victims of human trafficking. The physical effects may differ depending on the age of the victim and the type of work that a victim is forced to do.

If a person is forced into the sex trade, that person can come in contact with some very serious diseases. The most life-threatening diseases in the sex trade include HIV/AIDS and other sexually transmitted diseases. Even if victims of the sex trade are released, their bodies might be so affected by the abuse they receive that they may never be able to have children.

People who work in other difficult jobs, such as spending their days carrying bricks or other heavy objects, can end up with constant back pain. If they work in agricultural fields that use insecticides (poisons that kill insects), they might eventually die of cancer. If they work in factories in which the air is polluted with chemicals, their lungs can become infected or damaged. When working on construction sites that use loud machines, the victims can lose their hearing. Some meat-packing plants use people who have become entrapped by traffickers. The jobs in meat-packing plants can be very dangerous. The laborers are forced to work at a very fast pace. Because they use very sharp knives and other cutting tools, many of the workers end up with wounds or even severed fingers and limbs.

Under normal conditions, workers in many industries are given masks and clothing that protect them. They are also given lunch breaks and shorter hours of work. But people who are enslaved are given no protection. And often, when their day is done, they have no soft bed to sleep in. They have no bathrooms in which to take showers. They also have little food to help rebuild and nourish their bodies. In most situations, these exhausted, poorly fed, and unwashed workers sleep in close contact with one another. Therefore, if one person is infected with a disease, the illness will quickly spread. More dangerously, if one person has a potentially deadly disease, such as tuberculosis, an illness that affects the lungs, the tuberculosis could wipe out an entire group.

For children, the lack of proper nutrition is even more significant. Because children's bodies are still growing, if they do not receive nutritious food, they might suffer from stunted growth. Even if they are released from slavery and return to a more normal life, they may end up much shorter than they would have been had they eaten a proper diet. Another problem for children is their teeth. While still young, children's adult teeth are forming.

A child waits for her mother who is being forced to help construct a roadway in Bhutan.

Without proper nutrition, their baby teeth often rot. Their adult teeth do not grow strong.

Some victims are forced to take drugs. Traffickers might give the victims drugs so they remain passive and easily controlled. Once victims are addicted to the drugs, they will constantly want to do more. So, even if they are given a chance to escape, the victims might want to stay in order to have continued access to the drugs. Also, traffickers can use drugs as a punishment. They might take the drugs away until the victims do what they tell them to do.

Psychological Effects

Almost all victims of human trafficking are placed in a situation of high stress. They might be worried about families that they have left behind. They might be afraid of the people who keep them captive because they are worried they will be beaten. They could fear immigration officials and being deported. They could, in extreme cases, even be afraid of being killed. There is also the stress of the work they are doing. Working long hours and doing very hard work cause stress. When people are constantly stressed, their bodies do not react in healthy ways. Stress puts extra pressure on the heart and can cause heart attacks, especially in older people. Stress can cause stomach problems. Too much stress also breaks down a body's ability to fight disease.

Constant stress can lead to depression. Depression causes a person to feel a great sadness about everything in life. Depression robs a person of energy and makes that person feel he or she is worth nothing. A person who is suffering from depression might even believe that the only way to relieve this great sadness is to kill him- or herself.

In addition to depression, many victims of human trafficking suffer from guilt and shame. After they discover they have made a great mistake in trusting the traffickers, they may be ashamed for having acted so foolishly.

They may feel so ashamed that they are afraid to go back home, even when they are given a chance to do so. Or, if they are lucky enough to escape and return to their home, they may feel so guilty that they are unable to tell anyone what they have been through. This is especially true for people who were forced to have sex or people who were made to kill. Even though these people were victims, they blame themselves for the cruelties they have suffered.

In the case of children as victims of human trafficking, the psychological effects can be more damaging. Children's minds are more sensitive because they have so much to learn. Children are searching for answers about life. When the adults around them are criminals, they have no one else to learn from. They may believe that the criminals around them are showing them what life is all about. The criminals become the models that the children want to grow up and be like.

Everyone who is under the constant threat of pain or death suffers a sense of helplessness. They believe there is no way to escape the beatings or other abuses they suffer. Even when they are released, they might still suffer from nightmares or a lack of sleep. They might be constantly nervous. They might worry that every stranger who approaches them might want to kidnap them. They learn to trust no one. This is known as post-traumatic stress disorder (PTSD). Most people who have suffered

A former child slave teaches other young victims of human trafficking in Cambodia.

long periods of stress can also have panic attacks. Panic attacks cause people to overreact to situations. For example, a person who has not had a lot of stress in her life might hardly notice the sound of a slamming door. On the other hand, a person who has suffered through long periods of stress might scream and run away when he hears a door slamming. The victim of slavery may feel constantly on edge, afraid that he is going to be beaten again, even though he is now safe. Getting over these fears may take a long time.

Social Effects

There are also social effects of human trafficking that must be considered. Some social effects include the loss of family support. This is true both for children and for adults. Families help one another in times of stress. A child seeks comfort from her parents and older siblings. But when a child is kidnapped or sold as a slave, she has no one to turn to. She has no one to tell her what to do next. No one is there to help ease her fears. No one is there to teach the child about doing the right thing. When the child grows up, she might not know the right way to treat her own children.

The social effects work both ways. The victims are not the only ones who suffer in the society. The families of the victims are also stressed. One of the parents of a family might have become enslaved by a trafficker. The rest of the family might worry about where that parent is and how that parent is doing. Children might especially miss one of their parents. They might become angry and afraid. When the children go out into the community, they might take that anger out on their friends. Fights might break out. And so the stress passes through the whole neighborhood.

One of the things that keeps a society together is tradition. Traditions are like stories handed down from one generation to the next. When someone is taken from a society, this can cause a break in tradition. A father who is missing from a family cannot tell his children stories about his past. He cannot tell them what their grandparents did for a living. He cannot tell them what their community was like many years before they were born. So, this man's children will lose their sense of tradition and belonging within a multigenerational community.

A mother cries after being reunited with her child, who was rescued from human traffickers in China.

Children who are kidnapped may be living in an entirely different country and never feel like they fit in. They may lose the ability to speak the language of their parents. So, if they ever make it back home, they may not even be able to talk to them.

There are many effects that are caused by human trafficking. And it is not just the people who are enslaved who suffer from this illegal activity. If allowed to continue to grow, human trafficking can affect every single person in the world.

Who Is Working to Stop Human Trafficking?

UN.GIFT

AGENDA

THE VIENNA FORUM
to fight HUMAN TRAFFICKING
13–15 FEBRUARY 2008 | AUSTRIA CENTER VIENNA

www.ungift.org

HUMAN TRAFFICKING
A CRIME THAT SHAMES US ALL

There are hundreds of agencies and organizations working toward ending human trafficking. Some of these groups are located in the United States, but there are also many groups all over the world. Some of these groups are branches of a country's government. Others are private organizations that focus their energy and money on specific issues of human trafficking.

Some of the specific issues these groups cover include pressuring governments to make laws that protect children. Other groups work to protect women and young girls from the sex industry. Different kinds of groups work to save children who have been forced to fight in wars. People who are forced to work in factories are represented by still other groups. Although these specialized groups might focus on specific problems and victims, they all have one thing in common: they are working to stop this modern form of slavery.

U.S. Government Agencies

Governments are working together to create laws and to provide money to stop human trafficking. In the United States, several different branches of the government are taking their own specific approaches to do this.

The U.S. Department of State has set up a special agency called the Office to Monitor and Combat Trafficking in Persons. It is through this office that the annual "Trafficking in Persons Report" is issued. This report has studied the problem of human trafficking in more than 150 different countries. The report states what the problem is and what each country is doing to combat human trafficking. Then the countries are rated by how strongly they are fighting human trafficking. The first purpose of this report is to make everyone aware of the problems of human trafficking. The second purpose of the report is to encourage these countries to take measures to stop this illegal practice.

The U.S. Department of State also offers money to help some countries to pay for special programs. These programs help to protect people who are most at risk of becoming victims. Since people who are poor or who do not have an education are likely victims of human trafficking, these programs provide education opportunities and jobs. In addition, the U.S. Department of State

You can go online to learn how the U.S. Department of State is fighting human trafficking and read its most recent "Trafficking in Persons Report."

is working with other countries to encourage those countries to enforce international laws against modern-day slavery. The State Department also teaches other countries how to catch people who are trafficking in human slave labor.

In recent years, the U.S. Congress has enacted stronger laws against human traffickers, such as the Trafficking Victims Protection Act (TVPA) passed in 2000. This law ensures that traffickers are punished and that the victims of human trafficking are protected. The U.S.

Department of Justice is working to make sure these laws are put into practice. Both the U.S. Department of Justice and the Federal Bureau of Investigation (FBI) have hotlines that people can call for help if they are a victim or if they know of someone who has been enslaved.

PREVENTING HUMAN TRAFFICKING

U.S. president George W. Bush signed the Trafficking Victims Protection Reauthorization Act in 2005.

Helping victims of human trafficking is one service that the U.S. Department of Health and Human Services provides. Through this government agency, victims are identified, rescued, and assisted in their rehabilitation. This agency also helps to make communities in the United States more aware of the problem of human trafficking.

The goals of the various U.S. agencies tackling this problem are: 1) to prevent human trafficking through public awareness, outreach, and education; 2) to protect and assist victims by providing shelters as well as health, psychological, legal, and vocational services; and 3) to investigate and prosecute human trafficking crimes by providing training and technical assistance for law enforcement officials, such as police, lawyers, and judges.

British actress Emma Thompson displays a United Nations publication on human trafficking at the first-ever international forum organized to fight this global crime.

International Agencies

The United Nations is the largest and most influential international agency working to stop human trafficking. In 2003, members of the United Nations held what was called the UN Convention Against Transnational Organized Crime. From this convention, two protocols (sets of rules) were created: 1) the Protocol to Prevent, Suppress and Punish Trafficking in Persons, Especially Women, and Children (2003); and 2) the Protocol Against the Smuggling of Migrants by Land, Sea, and Air (2004). These protocols state that countries must fight against human trafficking by making this activity illegal. With human trafficking made illegal, countries have the obligation to arrest all criminals involved in the trafficking. The protocols also state that countries need to make their citizens aware of the problems of human trafficking. The United Nations encourages countries to work with one another to help in the struggle against these crimes.

In 2005, the forty-seven member countries of the Council of Europe met and created the Council of Europe Convention on Action Against Trafficking in Human Beings. So far, the majority of members have signed an agreement to actively work against human trafficking.

The Organization of American States (OAS), which includes countries of North, Central, and South America, held a conference in 2006 that resulted in guidelines on how to combat human trafficking for the organization's thirty-four member nations. In Indonesia and Australia, the Bali Process, a group of thirty-eight different governments representing nations throughout Oceania and Southeast Asia, are using their combined influence to combat human trafficking.

Non-Governmental Organizations

There are many organizations that work to stop human trafficking. Some of the largest ones include Amnesty International, the Polaris Project, the Coalition to Abolish Slavery & Trafficking (CAST), and Free the Slaves. There are many, many more throughout the world. These organizations encourage governments to create new laws that will help the victims of trafficking or impose heavier punishments on the criminals. Some organizations aim to rescue victims. Other organizations work to educate the public about the problem of human trafficking and how to stop it. Still others, like Community Action Against Trafficking, which is based in Florida, help people in the community to recognize victims so they can be helped.

Outlook

Despite the actions of government agencies and non-governmental organizations, the United Nations reports

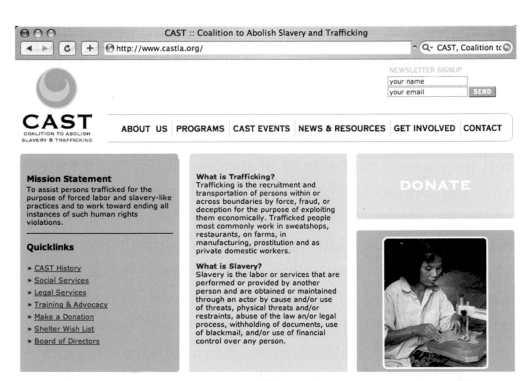

The Coalition to Abolish Slavery & Trafficking (CAST; www.castla.org) is one of several worldwide organizations that helps to fight human trafficking and assist its victims.

that the problem of human trafficking is getting worse. One of the reasons is that in most countries, criminals involved in human trafficking are more organized than the people who are trying to stop them. Laws may have been passed, but they have to be enforced in order for them to work as designed. Some countries do not have enough officials or money to go after the criminals. Other countries have not yet recognized human trafficking as a serious problem. Still other countries often deport foreign victims who have entered the country illegally.

In other words, they send the victims back to their home countries but do not try to help them. They also do not use information provided by the victims to pursue and punish the victimizers.

Whenever the world economy worsens, people often find they are in more need of money. The prediction from the United Nations is that as poverty and lack of education increase, the problem of human trafficking will continue to rapidly spread in the coming years. Although human trafficking occurs in every country of the world, including the United States, some countries are more susceptible to this crime. Poverty and unemployment in these places make people more vulnerable. Some of the hardest-hit places in the world for human trafficking are in Southeast Asia, especially Indonesia and Thailand. Countries in Africa are also plagued by high levels of human trafficking activity. Cities in the United States where human trafficking is high include New York, Dallas, San Francisco, Los Angeles, and Atlanta.

How You Can Help Stop Human Trafficking

When you realize that global human trafficking is the second-largest criminal activity in the world, it might seem like too big of a problem for one person to take on and make a significant difference. But if you read books on human trafficking or visit a Web site of an organization that is dedicated to solving the problems of this crime, you will see that anyone can make a difference.

There are steps anyone can take toward getting rid of this problem and helping the victims of human trafficking:

1. Educate Yourself

Read information online about human trafficking so you can learn more about where this crime is happening. You can also find books in the library about human trafficking. Talk to your teacher and ask questions about human trafficking.

2. Spread the Word

Start a human trafficking awareness group at your school, your house of worship, or your community center. Ask one of your teachers to sponsor the group. Or, ask one of your teachers to lead a lesson in the classroom on human trafficking. One of the activities you might do with your group is to create posters that call attention to this problem. Or, you could make bumper stickers with a slogan that reads "Stop Human Trafficking." You might also make bracelets stamped with this slogan and sell them in your community. Then you can turn any profits over to a legitimate organization that is working to help victims of human trafficking.

3. Volunteer

Find a local organization that is focused on human trafficking. Ask if there is anything that you can do to help in its work. You might type up letters or take mail to the post office. Or, you might be asked to do research on the Internet. Everything you do to help might eventually work toward freeing one more victim from a life of exploitation and slavery.

Anyone can help stop human trafficking no matter where they live or how old they are. All you need to do is connect with an organization, get involved, and get the word out.

Actress and activist Julia Ormond provides information about human trafficking to an International Relations Committee of the U.S. House of Representatives.

4. Give Money

Find an organization that is working to stop human trafficking and offer your allowance, birthday money, or part of your paycheck once in a while. Instead of birthday or holiday presents, ask people to donate money to the organization of your choice. Every little bit helps. If every student in your school gave just one dollar a month, that organization would have a few thousand dollars per year more to spend fighting human trafficking than it had before. Ask your parents or your teacher to suggest an organization that you can trust.

5. Write a Letter to Your Congressperson

Ask your congressperson what he or she is doing to stop human trafficking. Let your congressperson know that you want to stop this problem.

Myths and Facts

Myth: Human trafficking may occur in some places, but it's not a huge problem and doesn't affect many people.

Fact: The International Labor Organization, an agency within the United Nations, estimates that there are 12.3 million people trapped in forced labor, debt bondage, child labor, child soldiering, and sexual slavery at any given time. Other estimates range anywhere from 4 million to 27 million. According to U.S. government–sponsored research, about 800,000 people are trafficked across national borders every year. This does not include the millions of people trafficked within their own countries.

Myth: Human trafficking only occurs in impoverished and developing nations. Modern-day slavery does not exist in North America. Even if it does, it is a problem that only affects illegal immigrants.

Fact: According to the U.S. State Department's 2007 "Trafficking in Persons Report," the United States is both a source and destination country for thousands of men, women, and children trafficked for the purpose of sexual and labor exploitation. Women and girls, largely from East Asia, eastern Europe, Mexico, and Central America, are brought into the United States for the purpose of prostitution. Some men and women, responding to fraudulent offers of employment in the United States, migrate willingly and often legally but are then enslaved at work sites or in the commercial sex trade. An unknown number of American citizens and legal residents are trafficked within the country usually for the purposes of forced labor and sexual exploitation.

Myth: Victims of human trafficking would have even worse lives in their home countries if they did not have this work. They might not have understood what they were getting into, but they might be even poorer or even have died if they had not signed on for this labor arrangement.

Fact: Human trafficking is modern-day slavery, and its victims are modern-day slaves. They have not been "saved" or "rescued" from poverty by these "jobs." Victims have been stripped of their basic human rights and freedoms. They often suffer physical and emotional abuse, rape, threats against themselves and their families, document theft, and even death. The use of force or coercion by traffickers to maintain control over their victims can be physical, violent, psychological, and even fatal.

Glossary

admission Allowing someone to enter.

bribe Giving money or a gift to sway an official to perform a desired favor or action.

captor A person who has seized and held someone against his or her will.

consequence The result of an action.

desperate Having little or no hope, which might cause someone to do something dangerous.

devastate To overwhelm or to destroy.

enslave To make someone a slave; to force someone to perform labor without pay or freedom to quit.

entice To attract someone by raising hope and desires.

immigration The act of entering a country other than one's own in order to make a new home there.

influence To sway a person to take a certain action.

prey To victimize and exploit a person.

refugee A person who flees to a place of safety to get away from dangers at home.

rehabilitation The act of restoring something, such as a person's physical and mental health.

susceptible Especially sensitive and likely to be affected by something, such as disease.

transmit To pass or spread something along.

vulnerable Especially defenseless against something.

For More Information

Anti-Slavery International
Thomas Clarkson House, the Stableyard
Broomgrove Road
London, SW9 9TL
England
Web site: http://www.antislavery.org
This organization, founded in 1839, is the world's oldest
international human rights organization. It works
with governments, conducts research to assess the
scale of slavery, and helps local organizations raise
public awareness about the problem.

British Columbia's Office to Combat Trafficking in Persons
Public Safety and Solicitor General Communications Office
Victoria, BC V8W 9J7
Canada
(250) 953-4970
This group was begun by students at the University of
British Columbia. Their goal is to gather facts about
human trafficking in Canada and present recommen-
dations to the Canadian government on how to fight it.

Human Rights Watch
350 Fifth Avenue, 34th Floor

New York, NY 10118-3299

(212) 290-4700

Web site: http://www.hrw.org/about/projects/traffcamp/
intro.html

This group is called a humanitarian watchdog group. It
brings human rights violations, such as child slavery,
to the attention of the press, the public, other organizations, and governments around the world.

Stop the Traffik

132 Temple Street, 2nd Floor

New Haven, CT 06510

(203) 773-0602

Web site: http://www.stopthetraffik.org

This is a group of different organizations that are
spreading the word about human trafficking, reaching
activists all over the world. There are offices in many
different countries, including the United States.

U.S. Department of Health and Human Services

200 Independence Avenue SW

Washington, DC 20201

(202) 619-0257

(877) 696-6775

Web site: http://www.hhs.gov

This federal department has the elimination of human
trafficking as one of its goals.

Women's Human Rights Resources
Bora Laskin Law Library
78 Queen's Park
Toronto, ON M5S 2C5
Canada
Web site: http://www.law-lib.utoronto.ca/diana/index.htm
This organization researches the laws that protect women
in human trafficking. It offers courses on this topic
and invites student papers written on the topic of
women's rights.

Web Sites

Due to the changing nature of Internet links, Rosen
Publishing has developed an online list of Web sites
related to the subject of this book. This site is updated
regularly. Please use this link to access this list:

http://www.rosenlinks.com/itn/hutr

For Further Reading

Bales, Kevin. *Disposable People: New Slavery in the Global Economy*. Berkeley, CA: University of California Press, 2004.

Bales, Kevin. *Ending Slavery: How We Free Today's Slaves*. Berkeley, CA: University of California Press, 2007.

Beah, Ishmael. *A Long Way Gone: Memoirs of a Boy Soldier*. New York, NY: Farrar, Straus and Giroux, 2007.

Farnham, Kevin. *MySpace Safety: 51 Tips for Teens and Parents*. Pomfret, CT: How-To Primers, 2006.

Hunter, Zach. *Be the Change: Your Guide to Freeing Slaves and Changing the World*. Grand Rapids, MI: Zondervan, 2007.

Lewis, Barbara. *The Teen Guide to Global Action: How to Connect with Others (Near and Far) to Create Social Change*. Minneapolis, MN: Free Spirit Publishing, 2007.

McCormack, Patricia. *Sold*. Westport, CT: Hyperion Press, 2006.

Sage, Jesse, and Liora Kasten, eds. *Enslaved: True Stories of Modern-Day Slavery*. New York, NY: Palgrave Macmillan, 2006.

Bibliography

Bales, Kevin. *Understanding Global Slavery: A Reader*. Berkeley, CA: University of California Press, 2005.

Batstone, David. *Not for Sale: The Return of the Global Slave Trade—and How We Can Fight It*. San Francisco, CA: HarperSanFrancisco, 2007.

Bechard, Raymond. *Unspeakable: The Hidden Truth Behind the World's Fastest Growing Crime*. New York, NY: Compel Publishing, 2006.

Bowe, John. *Nobodies: Modern American Slave Labor and the Dark Side of the New Global Economy*. New York, NY: Random House, 2007.

Farley, Melissa. *Prostitution, Trafficking and Traumatic Stress*. New York, NY: Routledge, 2004.

King, Gilbert. *Woman, Child for Sale: The New Slave Trade in the 21st Century*. New York, NY: Chamberlain Bros., 2004.

Lee, Maggy. *Human Trafficking*. Devon, England: Willan Publishing, 2007.

Skinner, E. Benjamin. *A Crime So Monstrous: Face-to-Face with Modern-Day Slavery*. New York, NY: Free Press, 2008.

U.S. Department of State. "Trafficking in Persons Report." 2007. Retrieved April 2008 (http://www.state.gov/g/tip/rls/tiprpt/2007).

Index

About the Author

Joyce Hart is the author of more than twenty nonfiction books for students. Each time she writes a new book, she learns more about the world and the problems that face us. In writing about human trafficking, she has been inspired to support organizations that help victims of this serious crime.

Photo Credits

Cover (top left and bottom), pp. 4, 8, 17, 23, 25, 34, 37, 49, 52 © Getty Images; cover (top right), pp. 11, 13, 15, 19, 27, 29, 30, 31, 39, 40, 43, 44 © AFP/Getty Images; p. 5 © Popperfoto/Getty Images; p. 50 © Jeff Greenberg/The Image Works.

Designer: Tom Forget; Photo Researcher: Marty Levick